20.99

Iowa

THE HAWKEYE STATE

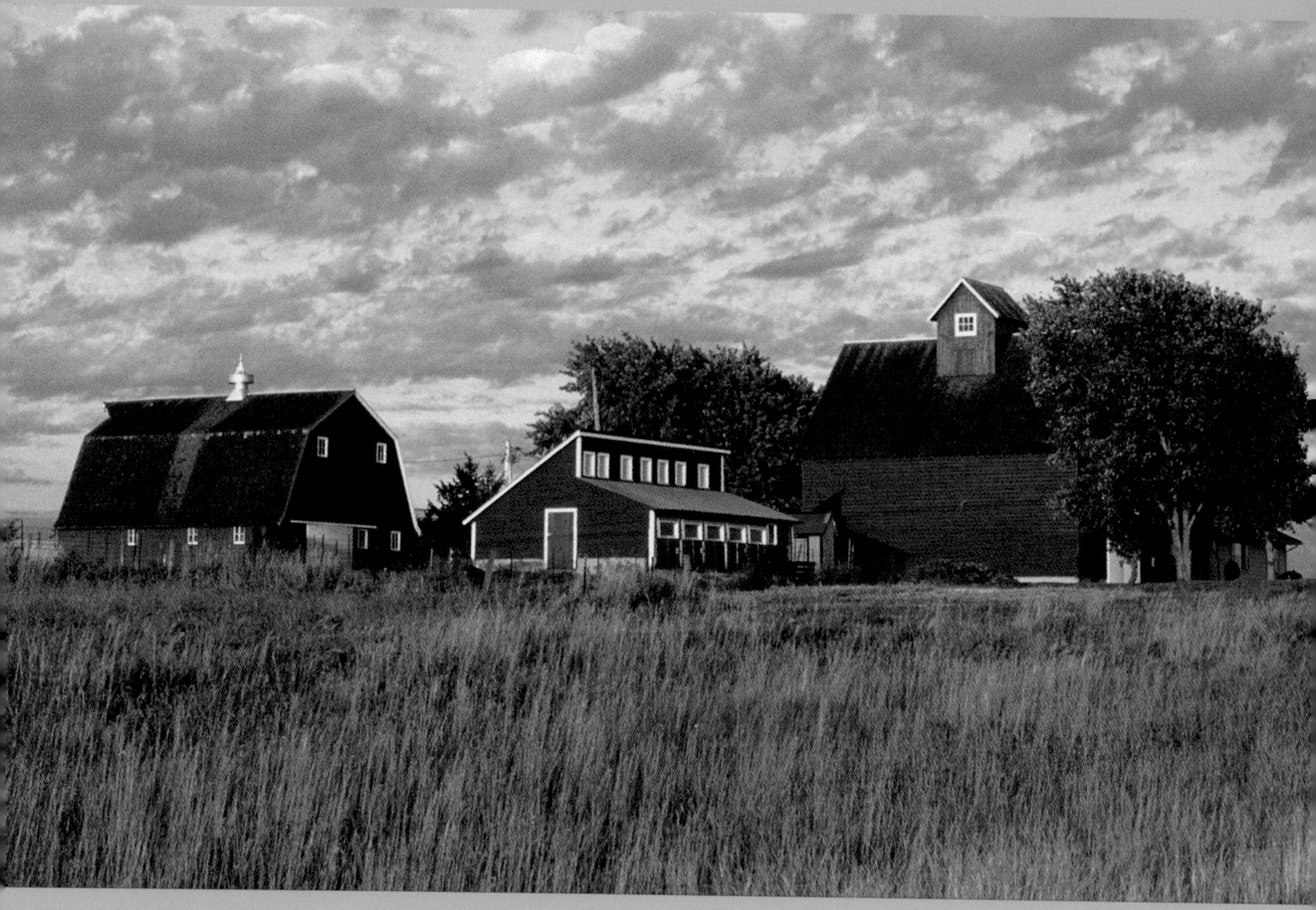

www.av2books.com

Go to www.av2books.com, and enter this book's unique code.

BOOK CODE

R153407

AV² by Weigl brings you media enhanced books that support active learning.

AV² provides enriched content that supplements and complements this book. Weigl's AV² books strive to create inspired learning and engage young minds in a total learning experience.

Your AV² Media Enhanced books come alive with...

Audio
Listen to sections of the book read aloud.

Key Words
Study vocabulary, and complete a matching word activity.

Video
Watch informative video clips.

Quizzes
Test your knowledge.

Embedded Weblinks
Gain additional information for research.

Slide Show
View images and captions, and prepare a presentation.

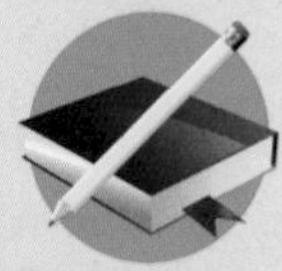

Try This!
Complete activities and hands-on experiments.

... and much, much more!

Published by AV² by Weigl
350 5th Avenue, 59th Floor
New York, NY 10118
Website: www.av2books.com www.weigl.com

Library of Congress Cataloging-in-Publication Data

Winans, Jay D.
Iowa / Jay D. Winans.
p. cm. -- (A guide to American states)
Includes index.
ISBN 978-1-61690-787-7 (hardcover : alk. paper) -- ISBN 978-1-61690-463-0 (online)
1. Iowa--Juvenile literature. I. Title.
F621.3.W565 2011
977.7--dc23
2011018328

Printed in the United States of America in North Mankato, Minnesota

052011
WEP180511

Project Coordinator Jordan McGill
Art Director Terry Paulhus

Photo Credits
Every reasonable effort has been made to trace ownership and to obtain permission to reprint copyright material. The publishers would be pleased to have any errors or omissions brought to their attention so that they may be corrected in subsequent printings.

Weigl acknowledges Getty Images as its primary image supplier for this title.

Contents

The location of Des Moines on the Des Moines River was an important factor in the city's growth. The river provided a major commercial transportation route.

Introduction

Iowa is located in the north-central area of the United States known as the Midwest. It is a major farming state that plays an important role as one of the nation's main breadbaskets. Vast cornfields and massive hog farms have supplied the country with food for decades. Iowa is often described as "one giant farm," with businesses that handle all aspects of the agricultural process, from harvesting crops to packaging foods. Roughly rectangular in shape, the state has rolling prairie farmland that stretches from the Mississippi River on the east to the Missouri River on the west. Its rich soils nourish some of the most abundant crops in the world. At its heart, Iowa remains a very large collection of rural communities.

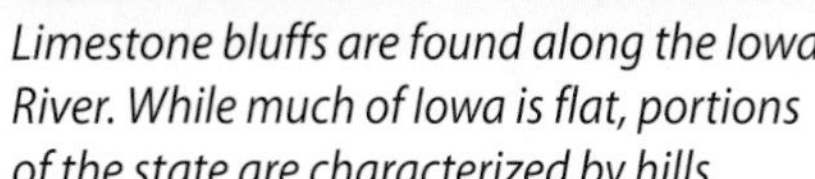

Limestone bluffs are found along the Iowa River. While much of Iowa is flat, portions of the state are characterized by hills.

Iowa is the one of the nation's leaders in soybean production. The state's farms produce a significant portion of the entire food supply of the United States and the world.

American Indians were Iowa's first inhabitants. French explorers arrived in the area in the late 1600s. Like many Midwestern states, Iowa was settled by adventurous people from the eastern United States as well as from Europe. The early American settlers often took over Indian land by force and claimed it for themselves. This led to many conflicts between Indians and white settlers.

An important **grassroots** political movement began in Iowa and nearby states in the 1800s. Iowans and others held small meetings in their homes to discuss their feelings about their region and the country. Instead of holding **primaries** to nominate political candidates, Iowans decided to hold meetings called caucuses. They still hold caucuses to choose U.S. presidential candidates. The Iowa presidential caucus came to national prominence in 1972 when it was rescheduled as the first nominating contest of the presidential campaign.

Where Is Iowa?

Iowa is located close to the center of the United States. For those traveling by air, Iowa has more than 100 public airports. Most of the state's major cities provide air service, but Iowa's busiest airport is the Des Moines International Airport. That airport and the Eastern Iowa Airport in Cedar Rapids are busy with freight cargo as well as passenger traffic. Railroads serve most of the counties in Iowa. In addition, a great deal of commercial traffic uses the Missouri and Mississippi rivers. Together, these two rivers provide almost 500 miles of navigable waterways along the state's eastern and western borders.

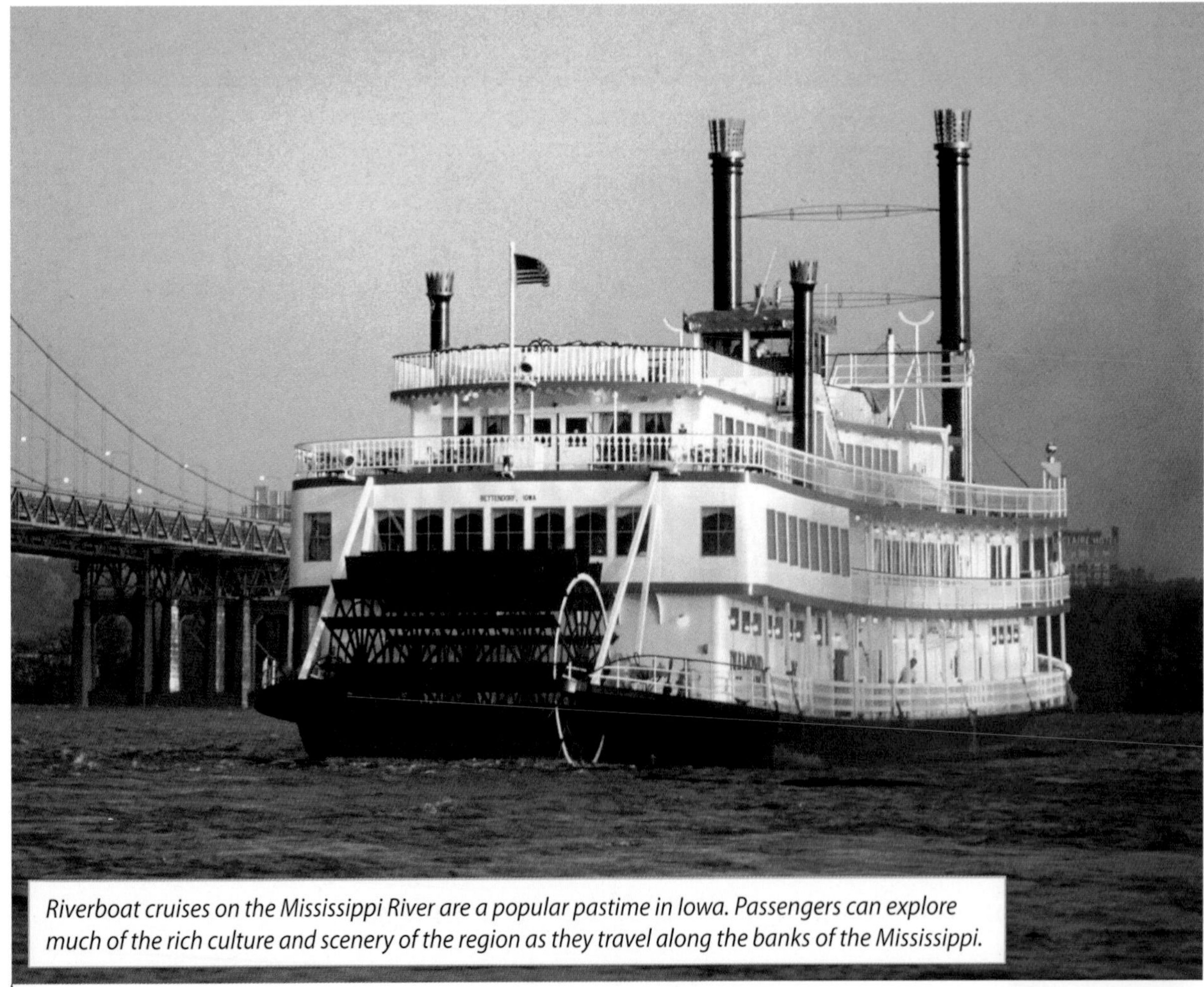

Riverboat cruises on the Mississippi River are a popular pastime in Iowa. Passengers can explore much of the rich culture and scenery of the region as they travel along the banks of the Mississippi.

Iowa suffered through devastating floods in 1993, 2008, and 2010. The 1993 floods were among the worst in the history of the United States. That year, some 23 million acres of land in the upper Midwest were covered with water for weeks. Other states, including Nebraska, Kansas, Minnesota, and Missouri, were also affected. After the floodwaters receded in Iowa, it was discovered that the pressure from the flooding had exposed underlying limestone, uncovering an ancient ocean floor. Hundreds of thousands of visitors flocked to the area to walk on the 375-million-year-old bedrock and search for fossils in the limestone.

Heavy summer rains have led to devastating floods in Iowa in recent years. Researchers say that the state's rivers and streams are running harder and faster than in the past, which also contributes to flooding.

I DIDN'T KNOW THAT!

"Iowa" is an American Indian word meaning "This Is the Place" or "The Beautiful Land." Both the state and the Iowa River were named after the Iowa Indians.

Clark's Tower, in Madison County, pays tribute to Iowa's pioneer past. Built in 1926, it is a 25-foot-tall memorial to one of the county's early pioneer families.

Although Iowa has been a state since 1846, its present boundaries were not drawn until 1857.

Iowa is known as the Hawkeye State, a tribute to Black Hawk, leader of the Fox and the Sauk Indians in the early 1800s.

The United States acquired the land that became Iowa from France as part of the **Louisiana Purchase** in 1803.

Mapping Iowa

Iowa shares its borders with Minnesota to the north, Wisconsin and Illinois to the east, Missouri to the south, and Nebraska and South Dakota to the west. Traveling through Iowa is simple thanks to the state's many roadways and airports. The state's rural road system connects its sparse population, which is spread over 55,869 square miles.

Sites and Symbols

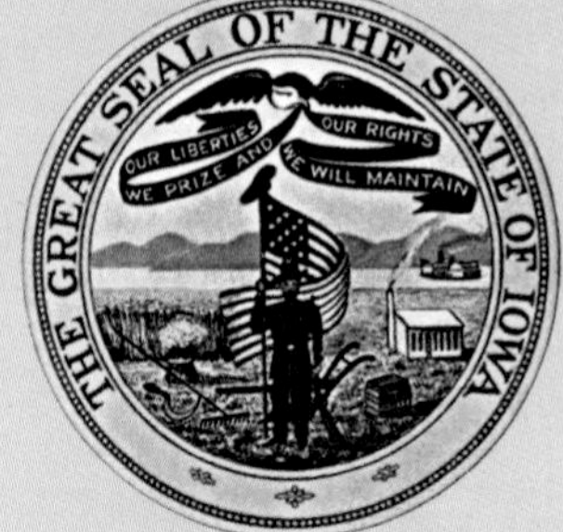

STATE SEAL
Iowa

STATE BIRD
Eastern goldfinch

STATE FLOWER
Wild rose

STATE FLAG
Iowa

STATE ROCK
Geode

STATE TREE
Oak

Nickname The Hawkeye State

Motto Our Liberties We Prize, and Our Rights We Will Maintain

Song "The Song of Iowa," words by S. H. M. Byers, sung to the tune of "Der Tannenbaum"

Entered the Union December 28, 1846, as the 29th state

Capital Des Moines

Population (2010 Census) 3,046,355 Ranked 30th state

MINNESOTA
WISCONSIN
SD*
IOWA
ILLINOIS
NEBRASKA
MISSOURI

Windom
Worthington
Jackson
Fairmont
Albert Lea
Austin
Stewartville
Spring Valley
Onalaska
La Crosse
Mauston
Viroqua
Milford
Sheldon
Spencer
Forest City
Osage
Cresco
Decorah
Sioux Center
Le Mars
Algona
Garner
Mason City
Charles City
New Hampton
West Union
Boscobel
Lancaster
Platteville
Belmond
Waverly
Guttenberg
Storm Lake
Fort Dodge
Cedar Falls
Waterloo
Dubuque
Galena
Sioux City
Sergeant Bluff
Sac City
Webster City
La Porte City
Monticello
Bellevue
Story City
Vinton
Onawa
Denison
Jefferson
Ames
Nevada
Marshalltown
Cedar Rapids
Marion
Clinton
Ankeny
Urbandale
Grinnell
Marengo
Iowa City
Eldridge
Blair
Missouri Valley
Newton
Williamsburg
Davenport
Des Moines
Moline
Omaha
Council Bluffs
Indianola
Muscatine
Oskaloosa
Bellevue
Ashland
Red Oak
Creston
Osceola
Albia
Ottumwa
Mount Pleasant
Wapello
New London
Galesburg
Shenandoah
Bloomfield
Burlington
Nebraska City
Lamoni
Fort Madison
Tarkio
Unionville
Memphis
Macomb
Maryville
Bethany
Keokuk
Falls City

*South Dakota

N

Map Scale

0 100 Miles

LEGEND

- Road
- River
- State Capital
- City
- Iowa
- State Border

STATE CAPITAL

Des Moines is the capital of Iowa. When Iowa became a state in 1846, Iowa City was the capital. Eleven years later, the capital was moved to Des Moines, which is located where the Des Moines and Raccoon rivers meet. Des Moines is also more centrally located in the state.

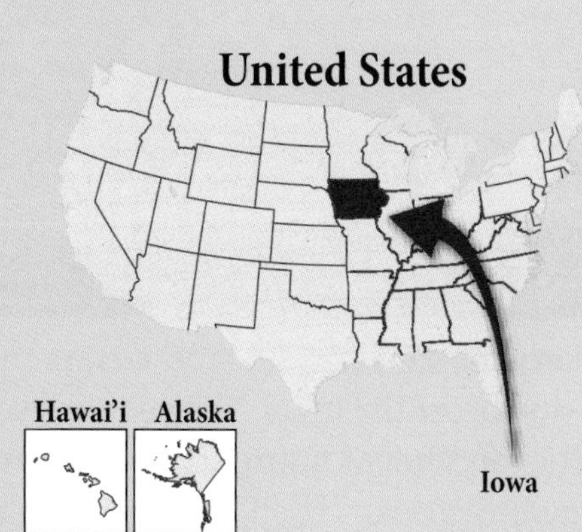

The Land

During the last Ice Age, huge **glaciers** covered the land that is now Iowa, as well as much of the Midwest. The heavy weight of the glaciers pressed down on the land, flattening it out. When the glaciers melted, the area was left with rich soil.

Today, Iowa has a prairie landscape of rolling hills and sloping valleys. It is part of the U.S. region called the Central Lowland. This is Iowa's only major land region. The Central Lowland consists of plains, hills, and excellent farmland. The soil in north-central Iowa is especially rich. Despite Iowa's generally flat landscape, parts of the state contain ridges, cliffs, and steep valleys. A **watershed** runs from the state's northwestern corner to its southeastern corner. Many streams and rivers crisscross Iowa, but the Mississippi and Missouri rivers are by far the largest in the state. These rivers make up Iowa's eastern and western borders. Other important rivers in the state are the Big Sioux, Des Moines, and Cedar.

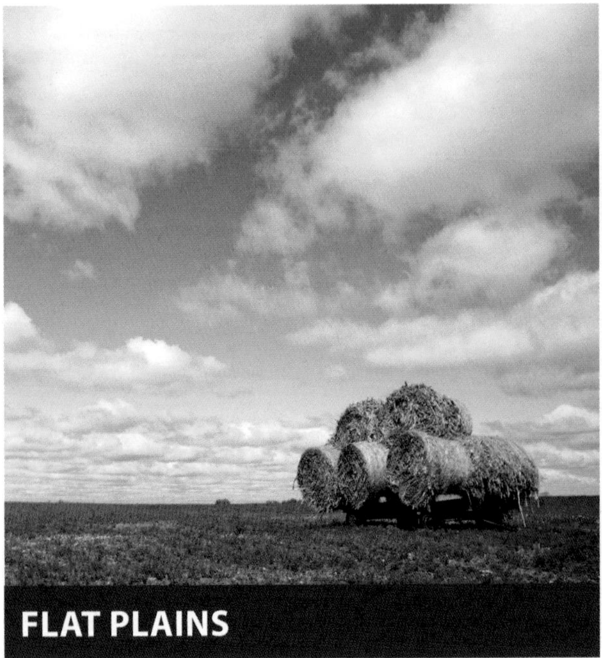

FLAT PLAINS

A large expanse of flat land covers much of north-central Iowa. The region's soil is fertile and full of nutrients important for growing crops.

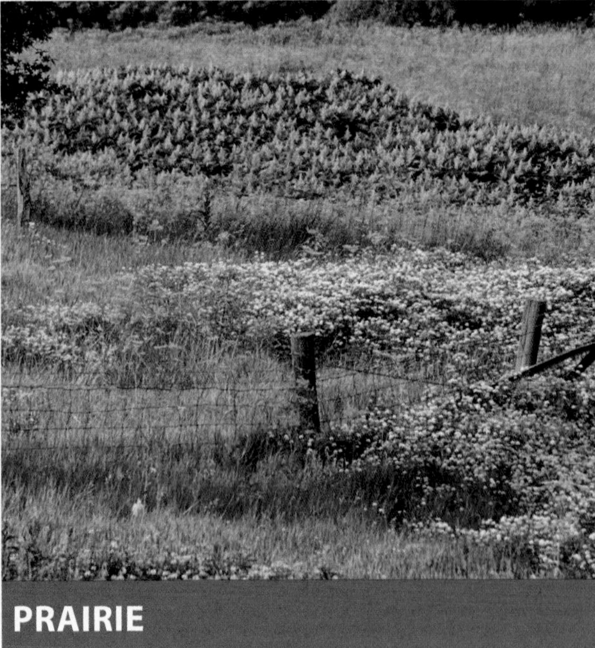

PRAIRIE

Vast prairies of grasses and flowers once covered much of Iowa. Residents have restored and reconstructed much of the prairie that was lost.

LOESS HILLS

The rolling Loess Hills in western Iowa were formed over a long period of time from deposits of windblown soil.

MALANAPHY SPRINGS STATE PRESERVE

Located along the Upper Iowa River, Malanaphy Springs was dedicated as a state preserve in 1994 because of its geological features, including cascading falls and high cliffs.

I DIDN'T KNOW THAT!

Iowa's growing season is about 162 days long. This is the time between the last frost in the spring and the first frost in the fall.

Iowa is the only state that has two rivers defining its entire western and eastern borders.

Hawkeye Point, at 1,670 feet above sea level, is the highest point in the state of Iowa. It is located on a privately owned farm in the northwest.

The lowest point in Iowa lies at the junction of the Mississippi and the Des Moines rivers. It is 480 feet above sea level.

Iowa receives an average of about 34 inches of precipitation each year, with less falling in the northwest and more in the southeast.

About 85 percent of thunderstorms in Iowa occur between April and September. June is the peak month for such storms.

Climate

Iowa's climate is extreme, with temperatures that sometimes drop below 0° Fahrenheit in the winter and soar above 100° F in the summer. January temperatures average 14° F in the northwest and 22° F in the southeast. Average summer temperatures range from 72° F in the north to 76° F in the south. The hottest temperature recorded was 118° F at Keokuk on July 20, 1934. The coldest temperature was –47° F at Washta on January 12, 1912, and again at Elkader on February 3, 1996. There can be severe thunderstorms in the spring and summer, with hail, high winds, and heavy rain. The state averages 46 tornadoes each year.

Average Annual Precipitation Across Iowa

The average annual precipitation varies for different cities across Iowa. Which city in the graph below gets the most precipitation? What problems might people have if their city got too much rain, and what could they do to solve these problems?

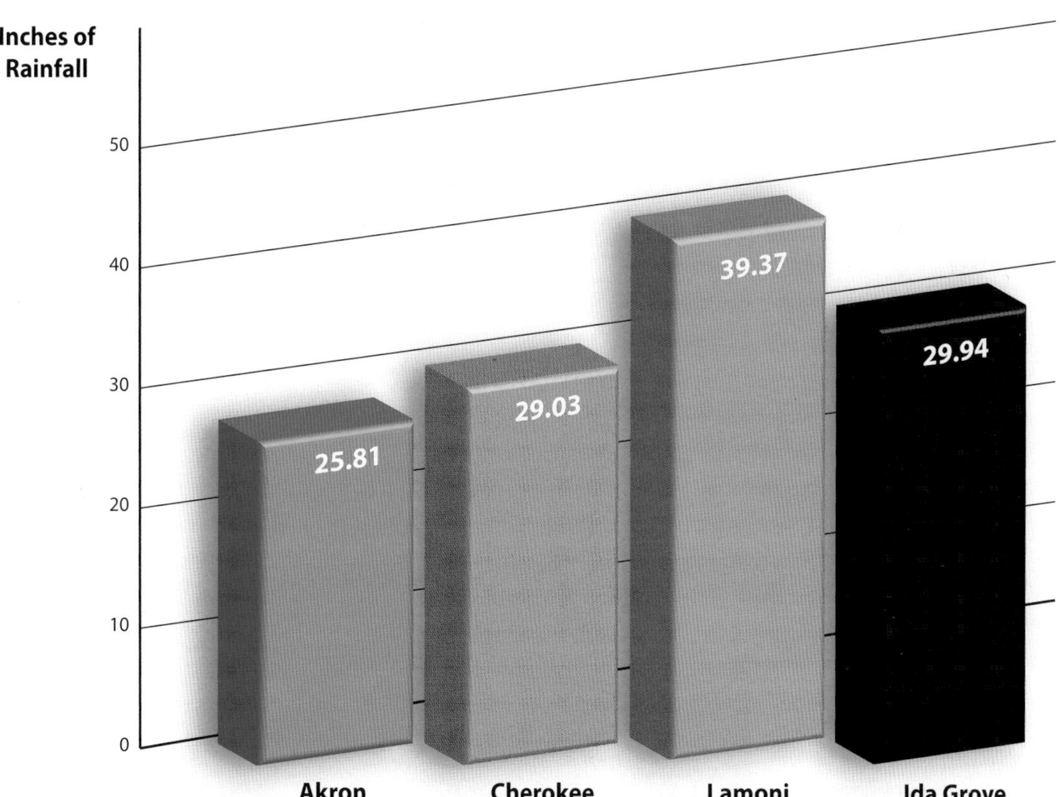

Natural Resources

Iowa's most important natural resource is its dark, rich soil. Massive ice sheets covered the area during different stages of the last Ice Age, which ended about 10,000 years ago. Each time the ice retreated, it left deposits of a material called silt, which is the basis for the high-quality soils. At one time, Iowa's soils were even more fertile than they are today. Over the years, overuse of the soil led to a decrease in productivity. In recent years, proper farm management and the development and use of **hybrid** crop species have once again increased productivity. Hybrid corn provides good **yields** because it is hardier and easier to harvest.

Iowa's rich soil, moist climate, and long growing season are major factors in the state's success in agriculture.

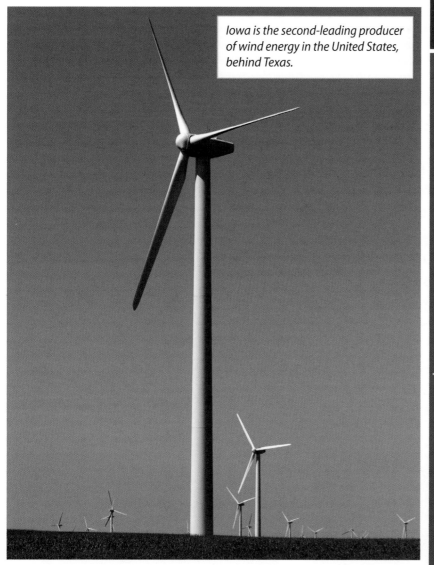

Iowa is the second-leading producer of wind energy in the United States, behind Texas.

Iowa once produced significant supplies of coal, and there are still coal **reserves**. Early settlers mined coal and used it for heating and cooking. Coal mining became an important industry, but production declined after the mid-1900s. Iowa still gets most of its electricity from coal-fired power plants. The state, however, has taken steps to harness its **renewable** resources, such as wind and solar energy. In 2007, the state created an Office of Energy Independence, which is charged with managing the Iowa Power Fund. The goals of this fund are to increase the state's energy efficiency and use of clean energy technology.

I DIDN'T KNOW THAT!

Tama, the state soil of Iowa, is one of the most productive soils used for agriculture. It is found in east-central and eastern Iowa, as well as in Illinois, Minnesota, and Wisconsin.

Iowa is one of the leading producers of wind-generated electricity in the United States. It is also a leading producer of **ethanol** and **biodiesel**.

Minerals mined in Iowa include lime and coal. The state also produces crushed stone, cement, sand, and gravel.

Gypsum, which is mined in Iowa, is used to make construction material and fertilizer.

The state rock of Iowa is the geode. The inside of a geode contains layers of crystals. Iowa is known around the world for its concentration of these beautiful and rare rock formations.

Plants

Many of the grasses and flowers that once covered Iowa's prairies were cleared to make way for new farmland. Some prairie flowers can still be found in ditches and roadsides across the state. Iowa's beautiful wildflowers include the pasque flower, aster, phlox, lily, and wild indigo broom. The state flower, the wild rose, grows throughout the state. Tall, thick fields of prairie grasses like the big bluestem once covered 80 percent of Iowa. These grasses still exist, but they are not nearly as numerous as they once were.

Many of Iowa's original trees have been cut down, but more than 2.8 million acres of forestland remain. The eastern red cedar is the only evergreen tree that is native to every county in Iowa. Although it no longer thrives in the same numbers as it once did along the Cedar River, it can still be found across the prairie in the **windbreaks** for farms. Other native trees in Iowa include the white pine, balsam fir, and common juniper.

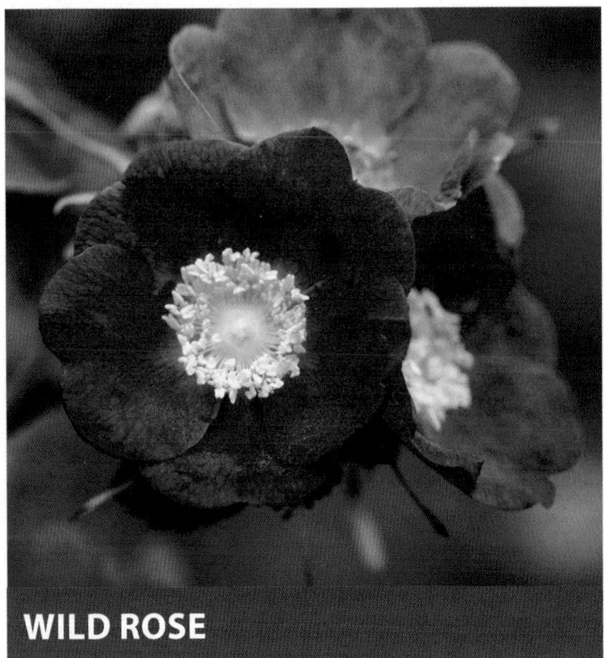

WILD ROSE

The wild rose was chosen as Iowa's state flower in 1897. The flower, which grows throughout the state, blooms from June through late September.

EASTERN RED CEDAR

Despite its name, the Eastern red cedar is not a cedar tree but a member of the juniper family. Its berries provide food for birds.

BIG BLUESTEM

Tall prairie grasses such as the big bluestem can grow to 12 feet high. This type of prairie grass once dominated the Iowa landscape.

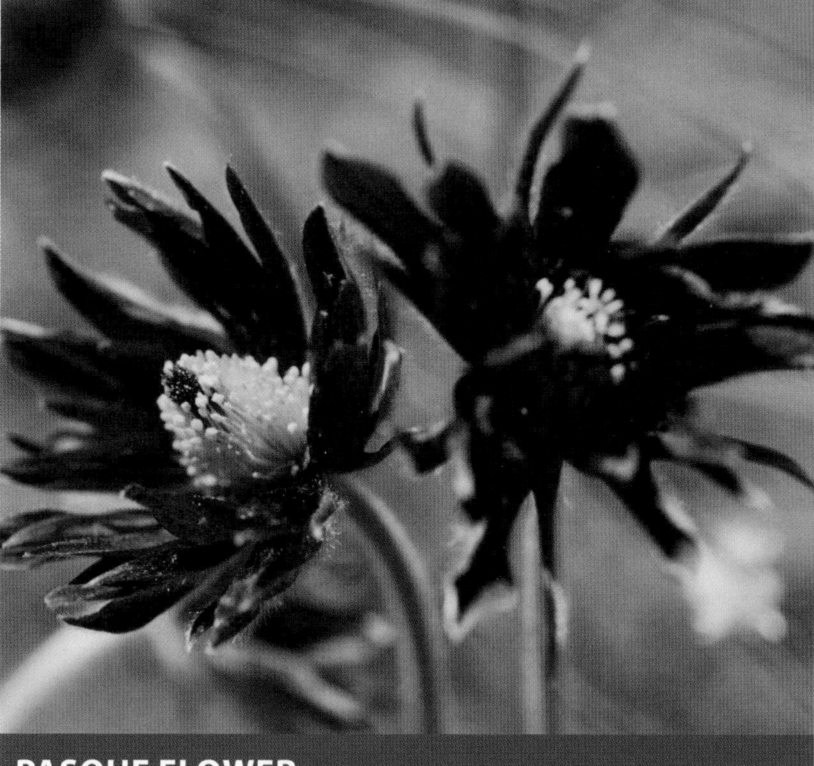

PASQUE FLOWER

This prairie wildflower blooms in March and April. Indians used its crushed leaves for medicine.

I DIDN'T KNOW THAT!

Trees common to Iowa include hickory, maple, elm, pine oak, and chestnut oak.

Thirteen species of oaks, including the black oak, red oak, and white oak, are native to the state of Iowa. Oaks are very valuable since their wood can be used in a variety of ways, such as construction, furniture, and paneling.

Nearly 6 percent of Iowa today is covered by woodlands. At the time the state was settled, as much as 20 percent of the area was forested.

A number of plant species in Iowa are threatened, which means they are in danger of dying out. One is the Northern wild monkshood, found only in the eastern part of Iowa and a few other states.

Animals

Iowa's animals include white-tailed deer, muskrats, raccoons, coyotes, and foxes. Other small animals in the state include opossums, skunks, groundhogs, rabbits, badgers, minks, and weasels. The most common snakes are garter snakes, fox snakes, and bullsnakes, though timber rattlesnakes are found in some areas. Timber rattlesnakes are very large, often reaching lengths of 5 feet or more. Since they are poisonous, they can be very dangerous.

Iowans can look to the skies for more wildlife. Crows, blue jays, cardinals, sparrows, doves, and kingfishers all live in Iowa. Bird-watchers can also spot migrating birds flying south for the winter or north for the summer. Iowa lies along the path of the Mississippi Flyway, which is a north-south migratory route used by millions of birds. Mallards, Canada geese, blue-winged teal, and redheads are among the birds that fly through Iowa.

EASTERN GOLDFINCH

The Eastern goldfinch, Iowa's state bird, is also called the wild canary. The bird stays in Iowa even during cold winters.

OPOSSUM

The opossum is found throughout Iowa. Adults can grow to 34 inches long. The average litter size is seven, but litters can be much larger.

WHITE-TAILED DEER

Deer are generally found in wooded areas. They also live in other places, however, such as marshes and grassy areas.

COYOTE

The coyote is found throughout Iowa. The animal eats a variety of food, including small mammals, birds, snakes, fruits, and vegetables.

I DIDN'T KNOW THAT!

When government official Joseph Street traveled through Iowa in 1833, he wrote that he had never ridden through a place so full of **game**. Iowa's prairies were home to many deer and other large animals at the time.

The ring-necked pheasant is an important game bird in Iowa. Other game birds are the quail and the wild turkey.

Many animal species that once lived in Iowa, such as the prairie chicken and the passenger pigeon, have become **extinct**.

A number of animal species in Iowa are considered **endangered**. They include the Indiana bat, the least tern, the pallid sturgeon, and the Iowa pleistocene snail.

Iowa's waters are full of smallmouth bass, trout, pike, and carp.

Raccoons and muskrats are still trapped for fur in Iowa today, just as they have been for hundreds of years.

Tourism

Iowa's natural beauty is on display to travelers throughout the state. Visitors can take a leisurely drive on the Loess Hills Scenic Byway in western Iowa. They can also paddle a canoe down the Inkpaduta Canoe Trail, which is 134 miles long and winds its way down the Little Sioux River.

Those interested in history can visit the Effigy Mounds National Monument to see the burial mounds created by the people who lived in the region thousands of years ago. Tourists can also retrace the journey of explorers Meriwether Lewis and William Clark along the Missouri River in the northwest in the early 1800s. On the other side of Iowa, tourists can visit Old Fort Madison, situated on the Mississippi River. At the fort, historic interpreters recreate life on Iowa's rugged frontier.

LEWIS AND CLARK STATE PARK

Located in Onawa, Lewis and Clark State Park features a full-size replica of the wooden boat that the explorers used to travel up the Missouri River.

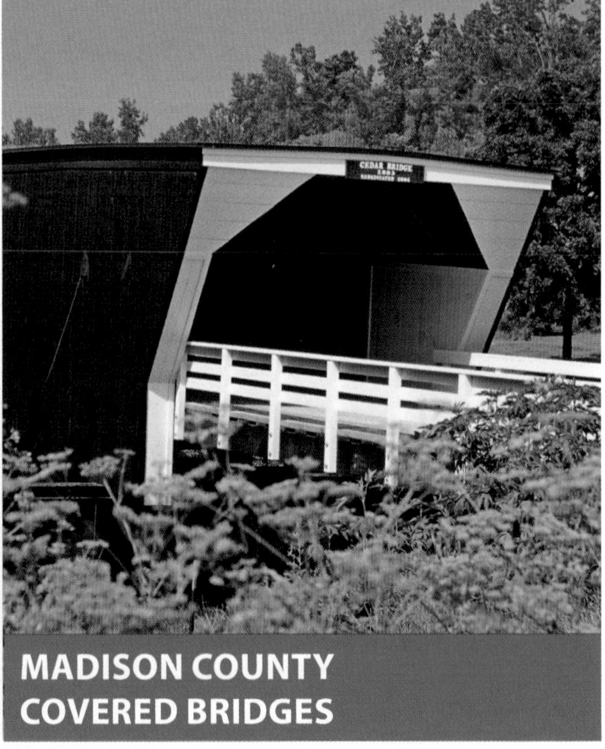

MADISON COUNTY COVERED BRIDGES

The popular book and movie *The Bridges of Madison County* turned the covered bridges into a popular destination. The six bridges are on the National Register of Historic Places.

***FIELD OF DREAMS* MOVIE SITE**

The 1999 movie *Field of Dreams* was filmed in Dyersville. The site attracts many baseball fans who visit the baseball diamond created for the film.

LOESS HILLS SCENIC BYWAY

The Loess Hills Scenic Byway is a series of roads running north to south in western Iowa. A variety of landscapes can be seen, including hills covered with prairie grass and wildflowers.

A reenactment of the Battle of Pea Ridge, from the Civil War, is a popular tourist attraction in Keokuk. Although the battle took place in Arkansas, many soldiers from Iowa took part on the side of the Union Army.

The National Balloon Museum in Indianola chronicles more than 200 years of ballooning.

Maquoketa Caves State Park has 13 caves, limestone formations, and miles of hiking trails.

Cross-country skiing is a popular sport along trails in Iowa's many state parks and forests.

The Grotto of the Redemption in West Bend is a site of religious **pilgrimage** for Christians. It covers an entire city block and was created by placing gems and colored rocks into concrete.

Industry

Industry in Iowa is closely linked to the needs of the farming sector. The earliest industries were based on mills used to grind wheat into flour. When the price of wheat dropped at the end of the Civil War, farmers turned to growing corn and to raising hogs and cattle. As a result, corn-processing plants and pork-packing plants developed. Creameries sprang up to process cow's milk into butter.

Industries in Iowa

Value of Goods and Services in Millions of Dollars

Iowa has a strong manufacturing industry, although other areas contribute more money to the state's economy. Why would wholesale and retail trade be an important part of the state's economy?

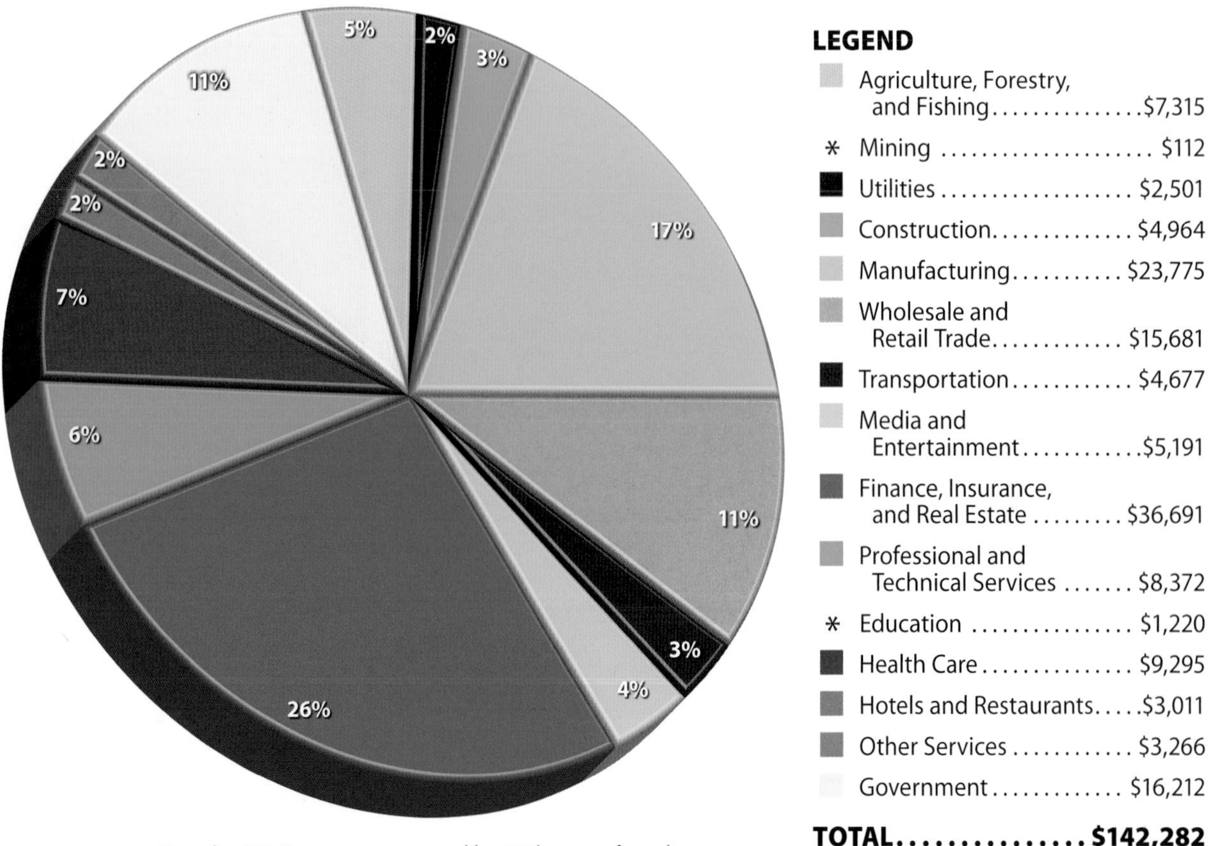

*Less than 1%. Percentages may not add to 100 because of rounding.

Today, Iowa has a strong manufacturing industry. In fact, manufacturing accounts for a greater percentage of Iowa's income than farming. Much of the manufacturing in Iowa is still directly related to agriculture, in the form of food processing and the manufacturing of farm machinery. Other products manufactured in Iowa include refrigeration equipment, laundry equipment, plastics, electronic materials, motor homes, rolled aluminum, writing instruments, and small appliances.

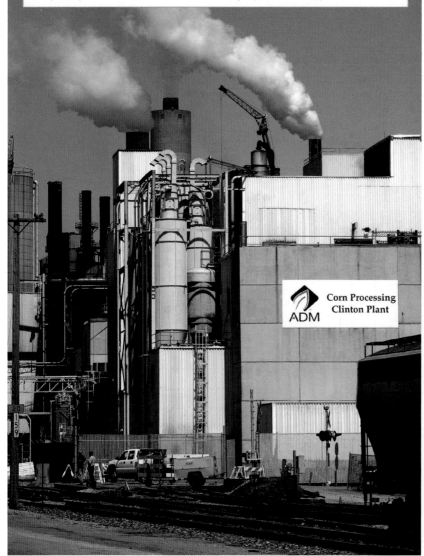

ADM, a worldwide company with 240 processing plants, runs a corn-processing facility that has been located in Clinton for more than 100 years. The plant processes corn into sweeteners, syrups, and other products.

The Duesenberg, a luxury automobile of the early 1900s, was invented and built by Fred and August Duesenberg, who ran a bicycle shop in Des Moines.

In 1939, John Vincent Atanasoff and Clifford Berry developed what is considered the world's first special-purpose electronic digital computer. They did their work at Iowa State College, which is now Iowa State University.

In the 1960s, Winnebago Industries began manufacturing large campers and motor homes, known as Winnebagos, in Forest City, which is located in Winnebago County.

Goods and Services

There are more than 92,000 farms in Iowa, and Iowa ranks among the leading states in the production of eggs, pork, corn, soybeans, and beef. The majority of the corn raised in the state is used to feed livestock, but some of it is used for making popcorn and other foods. Some of Iowa's corn is also used to make ethanol. Iowa corn is a hybrid corn, which is better suited to survive disease and drought. Soybeans also give Iowa's farmers a great yield. Soybeans are used to make food products, livestock feed, and a variety of goods, such as soap, cosmetics, and plastics. Iowa also has success producing several varieties of hay, including alfalfa, red clover, and timothy.

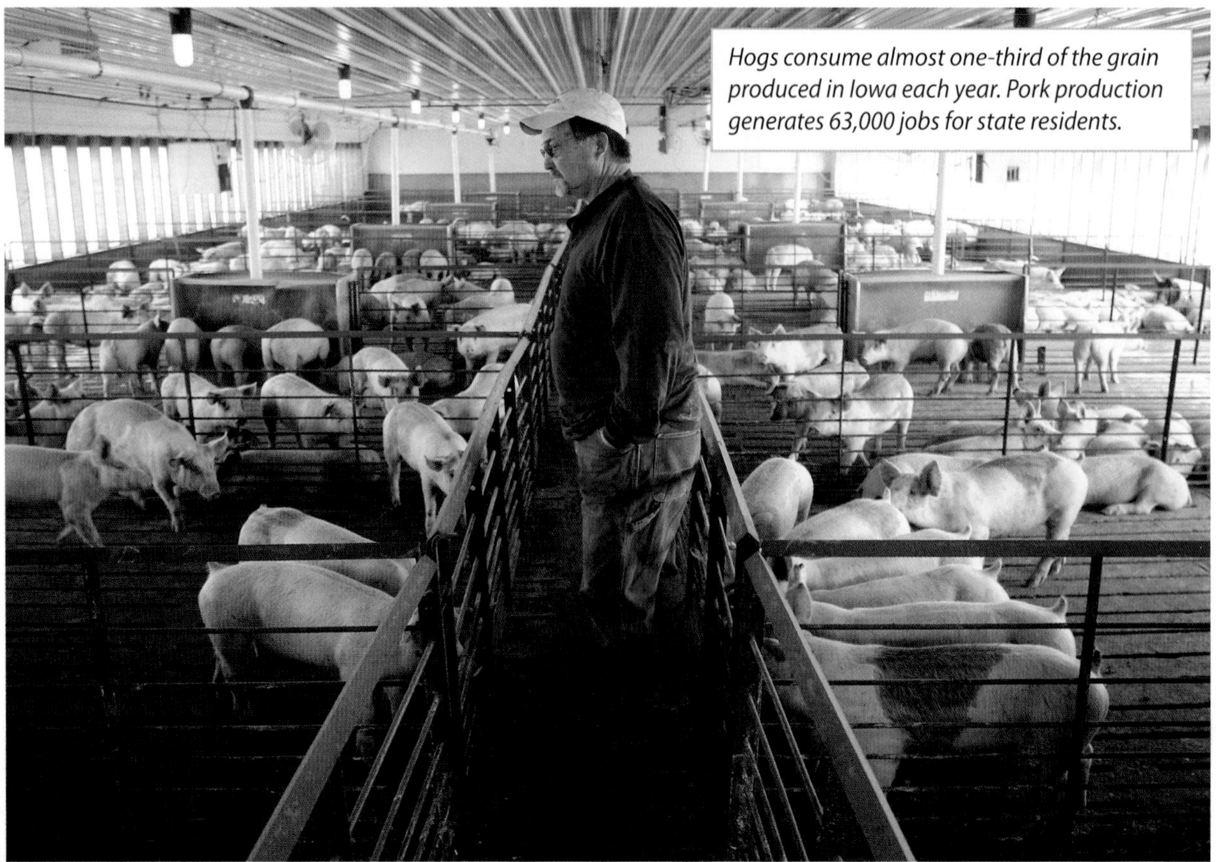

Hogs consume almost one-third of the grain produced in Iowa each year. Pork production generates 63,000 jobs for state residents.

Iowa is a national leader in the production of livestock and beef. In 2007, Iowa's dairy industry produced 4.3 billion pounds of milk, making Iowa one of the leading states for milk production. Most of the milk is made into butter and cream. Some farmers raise poultry and make their living from the sale of turkeys, chickens, and eggs. In 2007, there were 66.9 million chickens in Iowa, laying 13.9 billion eggs.

Government agencies, such as Iowa's Department of Economic Development, sponsor trade missions to encourage economic growth and to maintain the state's economy. Agriculture is assisted by research at Iowa's universities and colleges. Schools such as Iowa State University offer courses of study in agriculture and veterinary medicine. Despite the continuing importance of agriculture in Iowa, service industries now employ far more of the state's residents. Education, banking, health care, and insurance are important parts of the economy's service sector.

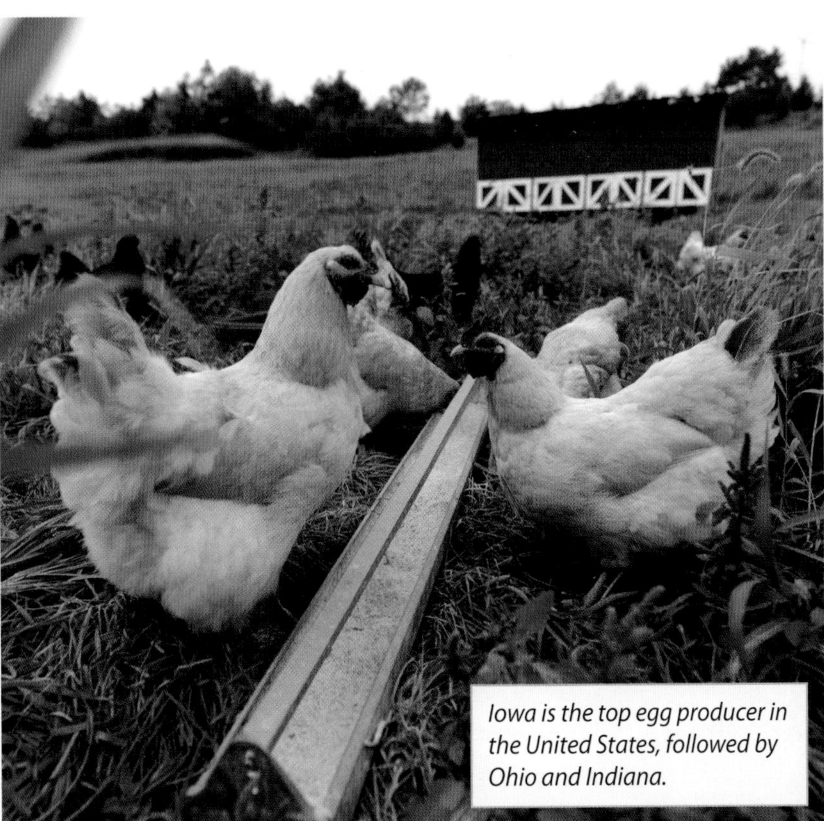

Iowa is the top egg producer in the United States, followed by Ohio and Indiana.

I DIDN'T KNOW THAT!

Iowa is said to produce one-tenth of the nation's food supply. In addition, as much as one-fourth of Iowa's exported farm products feed people overseas.

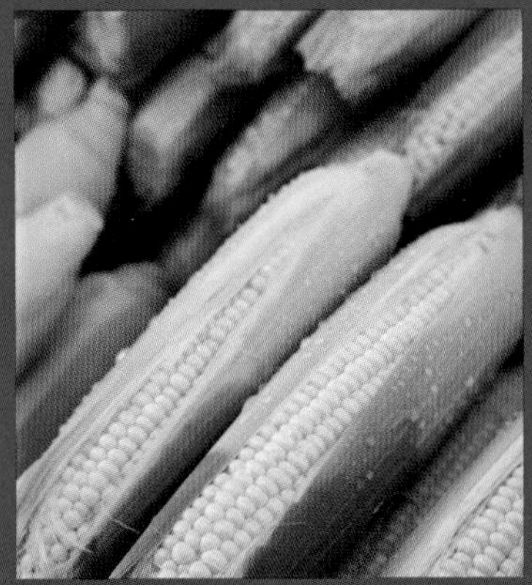

In 2009, Iowa farmers harvested 2.4 billion bushels of corn.

Wheat, oats, vegetables, and apples are all grown in Iowa.

Iowa is home to more than 19 million hogs and 4 million head of cattle.

Sioux City, Cedar Rapids, and Des Moines are Iowa's major manufacturing centers.

American Indians

The first people believed to have lived in what is now Iowa were the Mound Builders. They lived in the area between 2,500 and 10,000 years ago, after the last glaciers disappeared. The Mound Builders constructed huge dirt mounds that they used for burial ceremonies and for defense. They also left behind evidence of stone carvings, pottery, weaving, and trade systems.

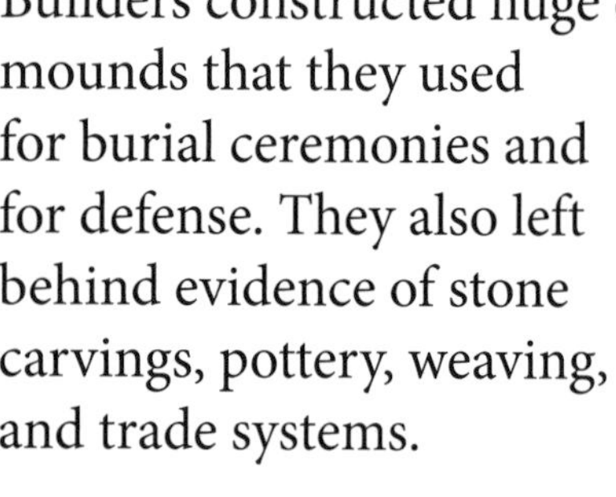

Keokuk was a chief of the Sauk and Fox Indians. He was in favor of making agreements with new settlers in the region rather than opposing them.

About 17 American Indian tribes lived in the area of Iowa at different times. One of the groups that once lived in the area gave its name to the state. The Iowa, or Ioway, people lived by both hunting and agriculture, using farming techniques that they learned from neighboring Indian groups. They grew corn and lived most of the year in permanent earthen houses. When they hunted, they lived in tepees. The Iowa spoke a language that was related to the Sioux language. They traded furs and clay pipes with the French.

After settlers began arriving in the region, the Iowa people surrendered to the United States following a series of conflicts in the 1800s. In 1836, they left their land in Iowa to the settlers and moved west. Today, the Iowa maintain a reservation along the Missouri River on the border of Kansas and Nebraska.

The Battle of Bad Axe, fought in August 1832, was the last battle of the Black Hawk War between Indian groups and U.S. forces. The defeat of the Indians led to increased white settlement in the area that is now Iowa.

I DIDN'T KNOW THAT!

Among the different American Indian groups that have lived in Iowa were the Omaha, the Missouri, the Sioux, the Winnebago, the Illinois, the Sauk, and the Fox, who are also called the Mesquakie.

Buffalo were among the animals hunted by the Iowa people. They also hunted deer, elk, turkey, and raccoon. They grew corn, beans, squash, and pumpkins and gathered wild plants such as mushrooms, nuts, and berries.

The Indian groups gave up their last official claim to land in Iowa in 1851.

In 1857, some of the Fox people who had left the state returned to Iowa and purchased 80 acres of land in Tama County. Today, the Fox settlement in Tama County is made up of some 3,500 acres of land.

Council Bluffs was the site of a historic 1804 meeting between explorers Meriwether Lewis and William Clark and American Indians.

Explorers and Missionaries

Father Jacques Marquette and explorer Louis Jolliet are believed to be the first Europeans to arrive in what is now Iowa. Marquette was a Catholic missionary born in France. In 1672, he joined an expedition headed by Jolliet, a fur trader who had explored and charted much of the area around the Great Lakes. The goal of the expedition was to explore the areas now known as Minnesota, Iowa, and Illinois. Joined by five other explorers, Marquette and Jolliet crossed Lake Michigan and the Fox and Wisconsin rivers. Then they followed the Mississippi River south to Iowa, where they arrived in June 1673.

In the early 1680s, French explorer René-Robert Cavelier, sieur de La Salle, surveyed the area. He was the first white person to voyage down the Mississippi River to the Gulf of Mexico. As a result of this exploration, France laid claim to the entire Mississippi Valley under the name of the Louisiana Territory, which included the land that became Iowa. Years later, when the United States purchased the Louisiana Territory from France, Meriwether Lewis and William Clark explored the land during their famous expedition.

Timeline of Settlement

European Exploration

1673 Father Jacques Marquette, accompanied by Louis Jolliet, arrives in Iowa and encounters Indians there.

1682 La Salle explores the Mississippi River and claims the entire region for France.

1788 Julian Dubuque establishes a lead-mining operation with the Fox near what is now Dubuque.

U.S. Exploration and Settlements

1803 In the Louisiana Purchase, the United States under President Thomas Jefferson buys from France the huge Louisiana Territory west of the Mississippi River, including what is now Iowa.

1808 Fort Madison is founded by the U.S. Army.

1832 The Indians lose the Black Hawk War, which leads to the opening of northeast Iowa to white settlement.

1834 Fort Des Moines is established.

Territory and Statehood

1838 The Iowa Territory is established.

1838 Burlington becomes the first territorial capital.

1841 Iowa City becomes the territorial capital.

1846 Iowa enters the Union as the 29th state.

Early Settlers

Julian Dubuque was Iowa's first settler of European heritage. He was a French Canadian who arrived near what is now the city of Dubuque in 1788. After receiving permission from the Fox, Dubuque started an operation mining lead. Dubuque hired the Fox to work in the mines. Dubuque and the Fox enjoyed good relations until his death in 1810.

Map of Settlements and Resources in Early Iowa

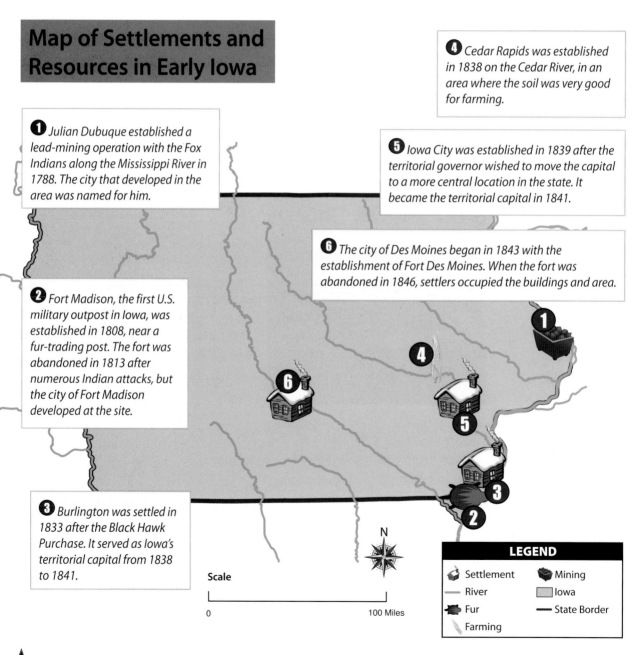

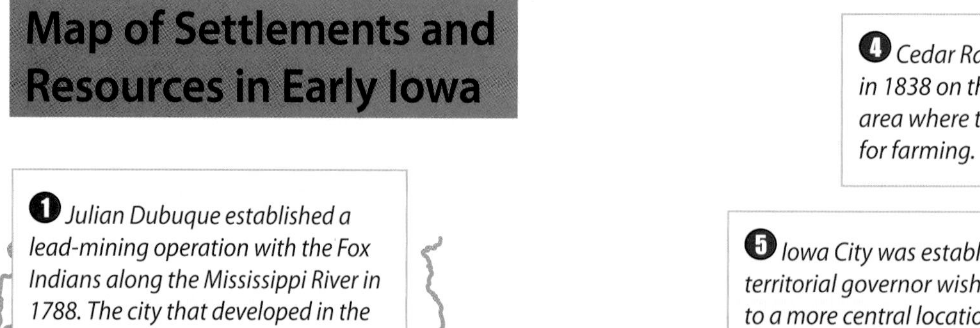

❶ Julian Dubuque established a lead-mining operation with the Fox Indians along the Mississippi River in 1788. The city that developed in the area was named for him.

❷ Fort Madison, the first U.S. military outpost in Iowa, was established in 1808, near a fur-trading post. The fort was abandoned in 1813 after numerous Indian attacks, but the city of Fort Madison developed at the site.

❸ Burlington was settled in 1833 after the Black Hawk Purchase. It served as Iowa's territorial capital from 1838 to 1841.

❹ Cedar Rapids was established in 1838 on the Cedar River, in an area where the soil was very good for farming.

❺ Iowa City was established in 1839 after the territorial governor wished to move the capital to a more central location in the state. It became the territorial capital in 1841.

❻ The city of Des Moines began in 1843 with the establishment of Fort Des Moines. When the fort was abandoned in 1846, settlers occupied the buildings and area.

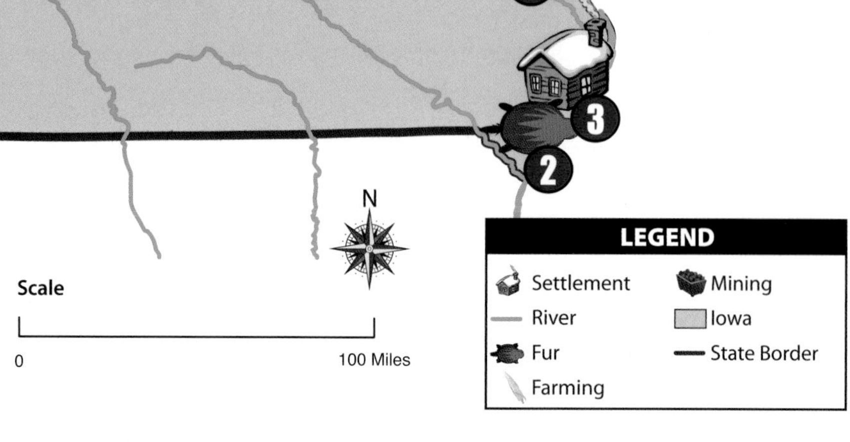

In the 1830s, settlers began arriving in large numbers from the eastern United States. They sought to take over land belonging to the Indians. In 1832, Black Hawk, the chief of the Sauk, led his people and the Fox in what became known as the Black Hawk War. The U.S. Army won, and the Indians gave the United States a strip of land west of the Mississippi, called the Black Hawk Purchase. White settlement then began in earnest. Before 1832, there were fewer than 100 white settlers in Iowa, but by 1840, that number had jumped to more than 43,000.

In 1835, when the U.S. Army sent soldiers to scout the Iowa area, the grass on the prairies was so high the soldiers could wrap it over their horses' backs and tie it in knots. The wild strawberries were so dense that they stained the horses' hooves red. Plowing the land for the first time was backbreaking work for the early settlers. The roots of the prairie grasses were extremely thick. When they were torn from the ground, it sounded like pistol shots. The early settlers farmed on 160-acre sections of land that were divided into quarters. The quarter sections formed an evenly divided grid of farms and small towns across the entire state. As a result of this land organization, most of the roads in the state run north-south or east-west.

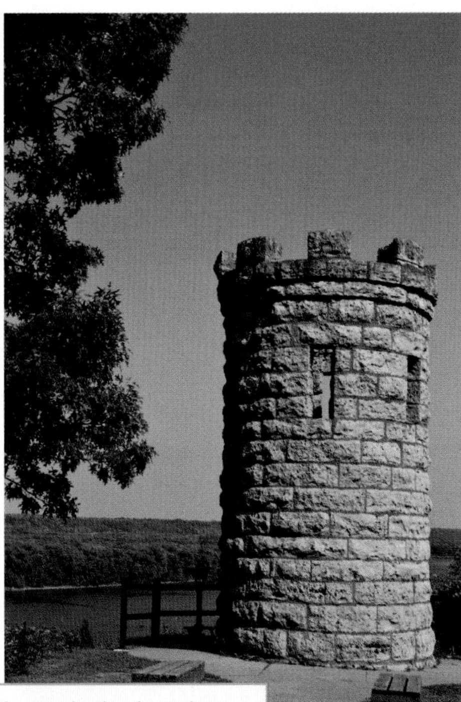

After Julian Dubuque died in 1810, the Fox built a burial site for him. It was replaced by a stone monument on the banks of the Mississippi River in the late 19th century.

I DIDN'T KNOW THAT!

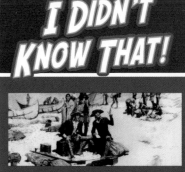

In 1804, Meriwether Lewis and William Clark crossed Iowa during their exploration of the Louisiana Territory. One of their companions, Sergeant Charles Floyd, died of a ruptured appendix near present-day Sioux City.

Before it became a state, Iowa was, in succession, a part of the Indiana Territory, the Louisiana Territory, the Missouri Territory, the Michigan Territory, and the Wisconsin Territory. It became the Iowa Territory in 1838.

In 1808, Fort Madison was built along the Mississippi River. The Sauk and the Fox did not like having a U.S. military fort on their land. The two groups joined the British during the War of 1812 and attacked the fort, burning it to the ground.

Iowa farmers planted rows of trees next to their houses to form a windbreak and give the homes shade from the hot sun.

Iowa's first library was established in 1853 in the town of Fairfield.

Notable People

Many notable Iowans contributed to the development of their state and country. Iowa can count many politicians, social reformers, and scientists among people from the state who made a difference in the world.

CARRIE CHAPMAN CATT (1859–1947)

Carrie Chapman Catt, born as Carrie Lane, moved to Iowa from her native Wisconsin when she was 7. She graduated from Iowa State College and worked as a teacher, school superintendent, and reporter. In 1887, she joined the Iowa Woman **Suffrage** Association. Catt became a leader in the suffrage movement around the world and played a major role in the passage of the 19th Amendment to the U.S. Constitution in 1920, giving women the right to vote nationwide. That same year, she also established the League of Women Voters.

HERBERT HOOVER (1874–1964)

Herbert Hoover was born in West Branch. He was orphaned when he was 9 and then lived in Oklahoma and Oregon. Hoover graduated from Stanford University in California and became rich running international mining operations. After World War I, he became a humanitarian, working with different organizations and helping people around the world. A Republican, he was elected president in 1928. The **Great Depression** began the next year, and his policies were criticized for not doing enough to help the country. He lost his bid for reelection in 1932.

HENRY A. WALLACE (1888 –1965)

Henry Wallace was born in Adair County and was raised on a farm. He graduated from Iowa State College and became an expert in plant **genetics**, developing types of high-yield hybrid corn and founding the world's leading seed corn company. During the 1930s, Wallace served as President Franklin Roosevelt's secretary of agriculture. From January 1941 to January 1945, he was Roosevelt's vice president.

NORMAN BORLAUG (1914–2009)

Norman Borlaug was born on a farm near Cresco. He developed a high-yield type of wheat that was resistant to disease. He also became a central figure in producing new types of cereal and improving crop management practices to feed the hungry people in the world. He received the Nobel Peace Prize in 1970.

JAMES VAN ALLEN (1914–2006)

James Van Allen was born in Mount Pleasant. He taught physics at the University of Iowa for many years. Van Allen was an important figure in the launching of satellites by the United States. In 1958, he discovered radiation belts around the Earth that are now called Van Allen belts.

I DIDN'T KNOW THAT!

Amelia Bloomer (1818–1894) moved to Council Bluffs in 1855. She became president of the Iowa Suffrage Association and was famous for wearing short skirts with baggy pants, which became known as "bloomers."

George Gallup (1901–1984) was born in Jefferson. He founded the company, now called the Gallup Organization, that collects public opinions on a variety of issues.

Population

The 20th century saw Iowa's population change from mainly rural to mainly urban. Many people moved to cities when farmers began replacing workers with machines. In the 1930s, about 60 percent of Iowa's people lived in rural areas. Now, about 40 percent of the people live in rural areas. Nevertheless, Iowa's rural population is still high by national standards. Des Moines is the only Iowa city with a population of more than 200,000. The next largest cities are Cedar Rapids, Davenport, Sioux City, and Iowa City.

Iowa Population 1950–2010

The population of Iowa has, in general, grown over the past 60 years. In the 1980s, though, the number of people living in Iowa went down. What factors would cause a state's population to decrease?

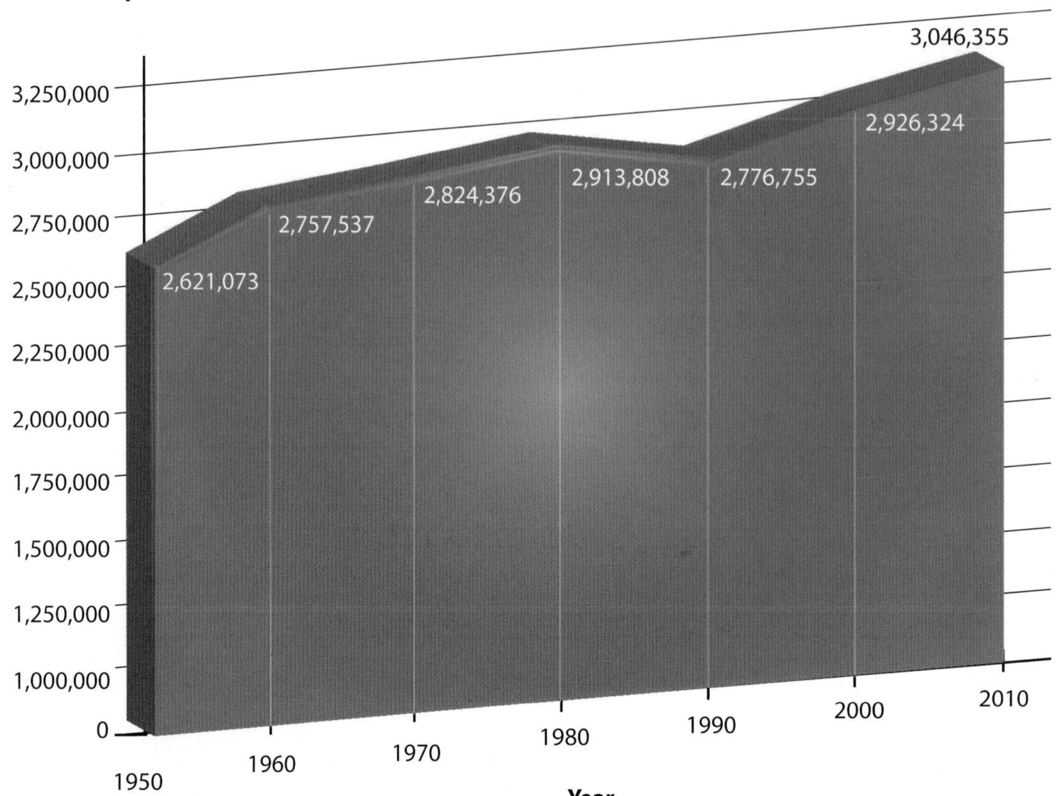

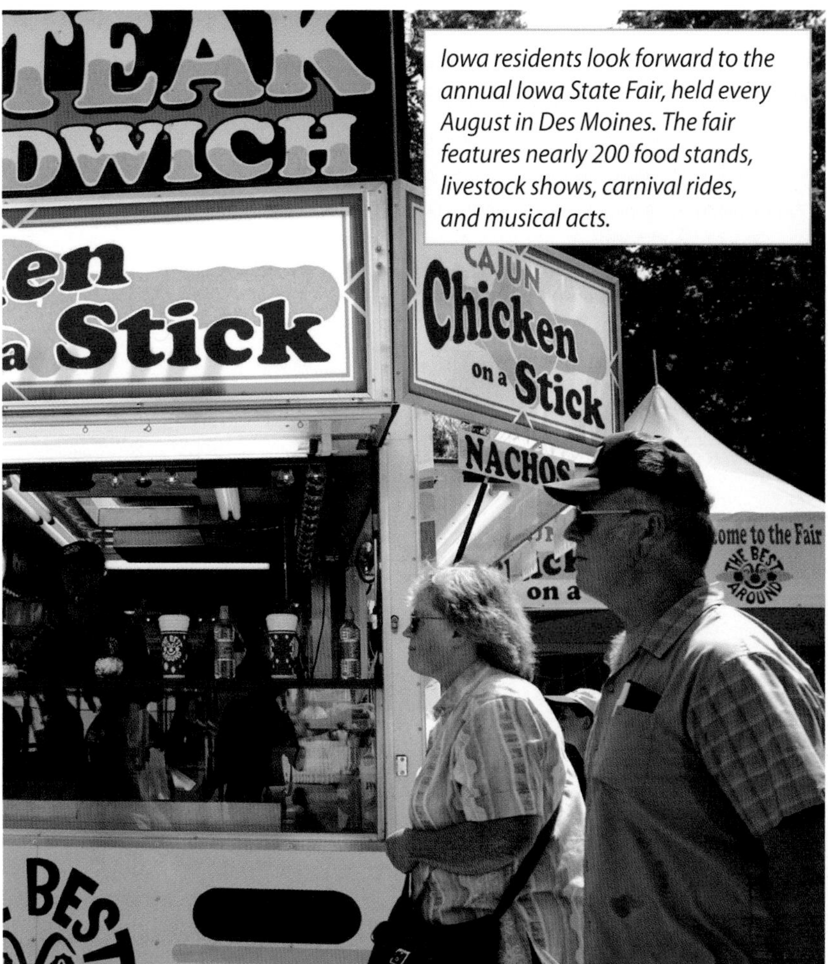

Iowa residents look forward to the annual Iowa State Fair, held every August in Des Moines. The fair features nearly 200 food stands, livestock shows, carnival rides, and musical acts.

Iowa's overall population declined during the 1980s. Since then, however, the population has increased. At the time of the 2010 census, Iowa was the 30th most-populous state in the country. It had a population density of 54 people per square mile, which was considerably lower than the national average of 87 people per square mile. Most Iowans were born in the state.

In terms of ancestry, people of European heritage make up the vast majority of the population. Less than 3 percent of the population is African American. Less than 2 percent is Asian American, and less than 1 percent is American Indian. Hispanic Americans, who may be of any race, make up almost 5 percent of Iowa's population.

I DIDN'T KNOW THAT!

After Iowa became a state in 1846, the population grew rapidly. By 1850, the state was home to more than 190,000 people, many of them European immigrants. Germans were the largest ethnic group, followed by the Irish.

Iowa has the highest literacy rate of any state in the United States, with more than 99 percent of Iowans able to read.

Iowa has three state universities. The University of Iowa, in Iowa City, was established in 1847. Iowa State University, in Ames, was founded in 1858. The University of Northern Iowa, located in Cedar Falls, opened in 1876.

When it was founded, Iowa State University was called the Iowa Agricultural College and Model Farm.

In 1855, the University of Iowa became the first state university to admit men and women on an equal basis.

The Iowa State Capitol, constructed between 1871 and 1886, is topped with a tall dome that is covered with 23-karat gold leaf.

Politics and Government

Iowa's government is based on its state constitution. Like the U.S. Constitution, the state constitution divides the government into three parts. They are the executive, legislative, and judicial branches. The executive branch enforces the laws of the state and includes the governor and other executives. The legislative branch is divided into the House of Representatives, which has 100 members, and the Senate, which has 50 members. Together, they form the General Assembly, which creates Iowa's laws. The judicial branch governs the court system. Seven judges rule on cases in the state's Supreme Court, which is the highest court in the state. There are also other lower-level courts in the state.

At the local level, Iowa has 99 counties. Each county is run by a board of supervisors, who are elected by county citizens. Iowa towns and cities also have their own governments, most run by mayors and city councils.

Iowa has elected mainly Republican candidates to office since the state's early days. From 1848, when Iowa first chose people to serve in the U.S. Senate, through 2010, Iowa has sent only 11 Democrats to the U.S. Senate, out of a total of 37 senators. However, Tom Harkin, a Democrat, was elected as one of Iowa's U.S. senators in 1984. He was reelected in 1990, 1996, 2002, and 2008.

Senator Tom Harkin still lives in the house where he was born in Cumming, a town with a population of less than 200.

I DIDN'T KNOW THAT!

Iowa's state song is called "The Song of Iowa."

Here is an excerpt from the song:

*You asked what land I love
the best, Iowa, tis Iowa,
The fairest State of all the
west, Iowa, O! Iowa,
From yonder Mississippi's
stream
To where Missouri's waters
gleam
O! fair it is as poet's dream,
Iowa, in Iowa.*

*See yonders fields of tasseled
corn, Iowa in Iowa,
Where plenty fills her golden
horn, Iowa in Iowa,
See how her wonderous
praries shine.
To yonder sunset's
purpling line,
O! happy land, O! land of
mine, Iowa, O! Iowa.*

Cultural Groups

In the second half of the 1800s and the early part of the 1900s, many immigrants moved to Iowa. These people included Germans, Irish, English, Scandinavians, Croatians, Italians, Dutch, and Czechs. In the early 1900s, African Americans from the South migrated to the northern and midwestern industrial states in search of work. Many settled in Iowa's larger cities, such as Des Moines and Waterloo. In recent years, new waves of immigrants have moved to the state to work in farming.

The settlement known as the Amana Colonies in the eastern part of Iowa was founded by a German religious community that migrated from Buffalo, New York, in 1855. Amana was one of the many experiments in **communal** living of the mid-1800s. In 1932, the people of the Amana Colonies voted to end their communal lifestyle. They reorganized themselves as a corporation called the Amana Society, which operated farms and factories. The Amana Church Society was created to maintain the group's religious beliefs.

Luther College in Decorah has an exhibit on the area's Norwegian culture. The college was founded by Norwegian immigrants, and students can take courses in Scandinavian studies.

Many Amish people in Iowa make their living by farming. Some also make furniture and quilts and run country stores and greenhouses.

Many Amish people live near Iowa City and Independence. The Amish hold beliefs that often conflict with modern technological practices. Their religious and social traditions include living simple lives without automobiles, electricity, telephones, or other modern conveniences. The Amish live in isolated communities and speak a unique type of German. The Amish are pacifists, which means that they do not believe in violence.

Lamoni, in southern Iowa, is the site of a **Mormon** community. The town was founded in the mid-1800s when Mormons passed through Iowa on their way to Utah to escape **persecution** in other states. Some Mormons settled in the area and established a community. Iowa is also home to members of a religious group called Quakers. The Quakers of the Springdale–West Branch area assisted with the Underground Railroad, a network of people who helped slaves escape from the South before the Civil War.

Elk Horn in western Iowa includes the largest rural Danish American community in the United States. The town has a Danish Immigrant Museum and a Danish Windmill Museum.

Nordic Fest is a three-day celebration of Decorah's Norwegian community.

The Dutch American community in Pella hosts an annual tulip festival.

The largest Amish community west of the Mississippi River is located in Kalona.

The African American Museum of Iowa, in Cedar Rapids, explores the history and heritage of African Americans in the state.

Arts and Entertainment

Grant Wood is perhaps Iowa's best-known artist. He painted local subjects in a realistic manner. Born in 1892 near Anamosa, Wood was one of the leaders of the regionalist art movement. Regionalist artists were known for their paintings of everyday rural life. Wood's painting *American Gothic* is considered one of the most recognizable paintings from the United States. Wood remained loyal to Iowa throughout his life and even taught art in the public schools of Cedar Rapids.

Iowa's colleges and universities are cultural centers that attract symphonies, dance companies, and musical shows from around the world. Iowa showed its commitment to the arts by establishing the first creative-writing degree in the United States. The Iowa Writers' Workshop got its start at the University of Iowa in 1936. Since then, the program has served as a model for other programs at universities across North America.

Artist Grant Wood got the subject matter for his paintings from his native state. The models for his most famous painting, American Gothic, *were his sister and their dentist.*

Actor Ashton Kutcher was a biochemical engineering student at the University of Iowa when he was discovered by a talent scout in 1997.

Some well-known performers have come from Iowa. John Wayne, a popular and rugged movie star, was best known for his roles in Hollywood Western films, such as *Stagecoach*, *Fort Apache*, and *The Searchers*. He was born in Winterset in 1907. Other performers born in Iowa include television talk show host Johnny Carson and showman William Cody, who was known as Buffalo Bill. More recent performers born in Iowa include actor and producer Ashton Kutcher, who starred in *That '70s Show* and *Punk'd*. Elijah Wood, who starred in *The Lord of the Rings* movies, is from Cedar Rapids.

Iowa has also produced a number of talented writers. Hamlin Garland, Wallace Stegner, Susan Glaspell, Elsa Maxwell, David Rabe, and MacKinlay Kantor all came from the state. Advice columnists Ann Landers and Abigail van Buren ("Dear Abby") were twin sisters from Sioux City. Meredith Willson, who wrote the popular musical *The Music Man*, was born in Mason City. The show is set in the fictional Iowa town of River City, which was based on his hometown.

I DIDN'T KNOW THAT!

Leon (Bix) Beiderbecke was one of the great jazz musicians of the 1920s. He was born in Davenport in 1903.

Glenn Miller, a trombonist and big-band leader of the 1930s and 1940s, was born in Clarinda in 1904.

In 1991, riverboat gambling was legalized in Iowa for the first time in any state.

The Ringling Brothers, who created one of the largest circuses in the United States, were born in McGregor.

The Kevin Costner movie *Field of Dreams* was filmed in eastern Iowa.

Sports

Sporting events are extremely popular in Iowa. Although the state has no professional teams at the major-league level, there are many lower-level teams. In addition, college sports are very popular. The University of Iowa's sports teams, called the Hawkeyes, draw large crowds. Hawkeye football and basketball games are especially popular. The Hawkeyes are not just athletes. They also excel in class. Students who participate in athletics at the University of Iowa have been notable for achieving academic success.

Many other Iowa colleges and universities have their own popular athletic programs. The Drake University Bulldogs regularly do well in a variety of sports, including football, basketball, soccer, softball, volleyball, and track. Drake University hosts the annual Drake Relays, one of the premier track and field meets in the Midwest.

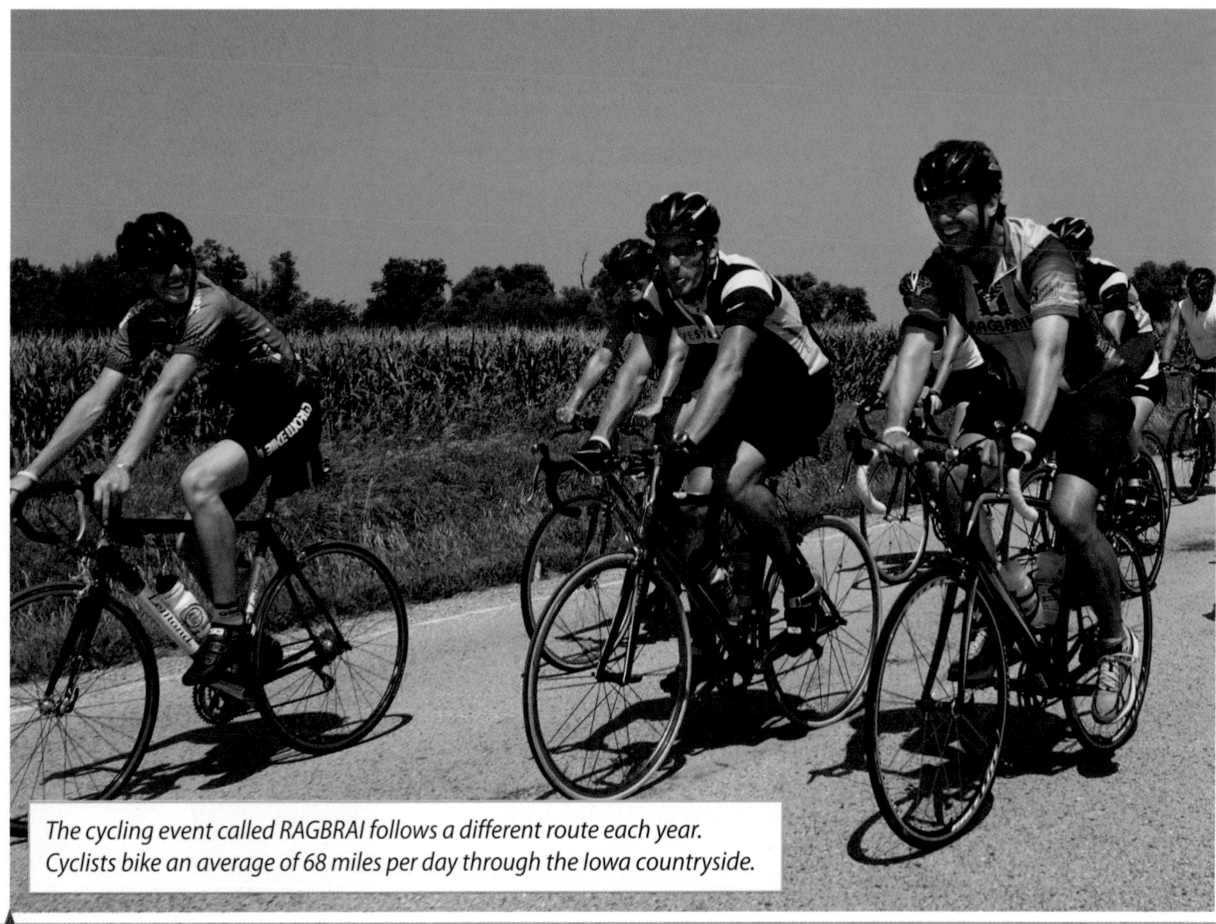

The cycling event called RAGBRAI follows a different route each year. Cyclists bike an average of 68 miles per day through the Iowa countryside.

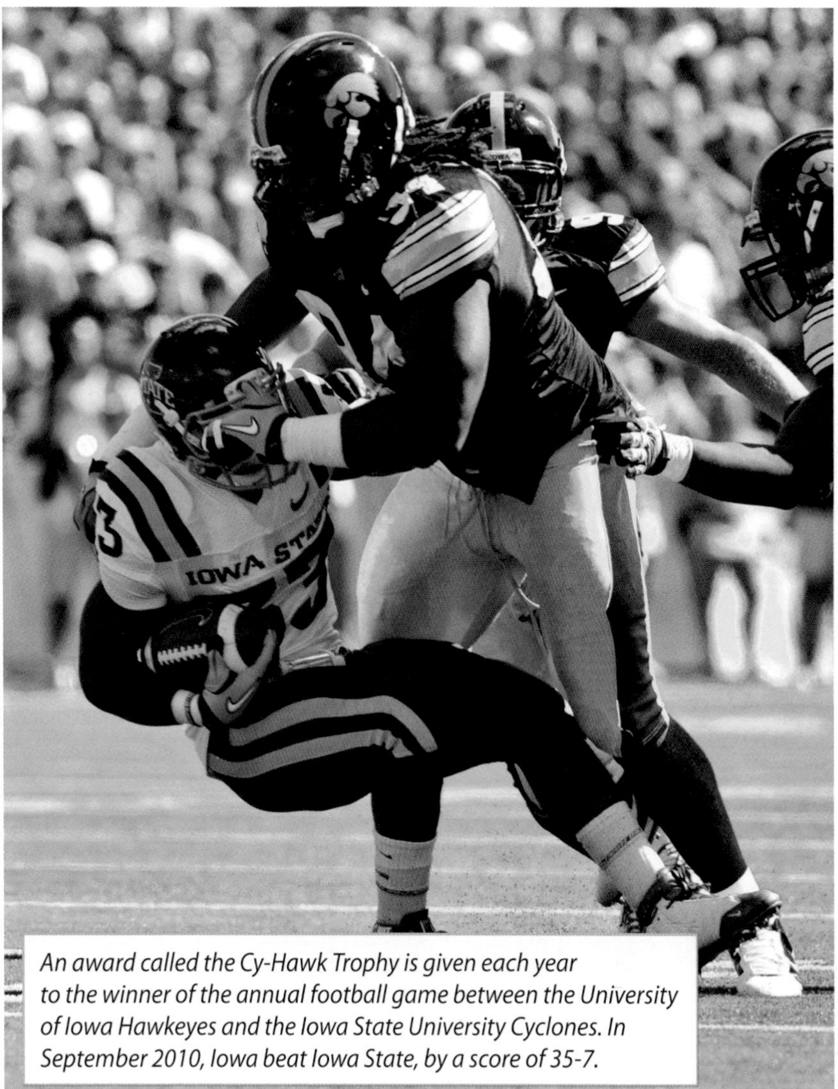

An award called the Cy-Hawk Trophy is given each year to the winner of the annual football game between the University of Iowa Hawkeyes and the Iowa State University Cyclones. In September 2010, Iowa beat Iowa State, by a score of 35-7.

Every year, the *Des Moines Register* sponsors RAGBRAI, which stands for the Register's Annual Great Bicycle Ride Across Iowa. This seven-day event, which began in 1973, is now the world's oldest, longest, and largest bicycle touring event. The ride begins in a town in western Iowa and ends in a town in eastern Iowa, with stops along the way. Since the event is so popular, those wishing to participate must apply.

Iowans participate in outdoor sports such as hunting, fishing, boating, and camping. More than 80 state parks and recreation areas provide residents and visitors with places to hike, cycle, and enjoy water sports.

I DIDN'T KNOW THAT!

Many outstanding wrestlers have come from Iowa. Frank Gotch, who was born in Humboldt, was the world heavyweight wrestling champion from 1908 to 1915.

The Hawkeye wrestling team at the University of Iowa has won the national college championship more than 20 times, including 2008, 2009, and 2010.

Hall of Fame member and fastball pitcher Bob Feller was born and raised in Van Meter. He began playing with the Cleveland Indians in 1936, at the age of 17. He won 266 games and had 2,581 strikeouts in a 20-year career interrupted by service in the navy during World War II.

Dan Gable, who was born in Waterloo and was an outstanding wrestling coach at the University of Iowa from 1977 to 1997, won a gold medal at the Olympic Games in 1972.

National Averages Comparison

The United States is a federal republic, consisting of fifty states and the District of Columbia. Alaska and Hawai'i are the only non-contiguous, or non-touching, states in the nation. Today, the United States of America is the third-largest country in the world in population. The United States Census Bureau takes a census, or count of all the people, every ten years. It also regularly collects other kinds of data about the population and the economy. How does Iowa compare to the national average?

Comparison Chart

United States 2010 Census Data *	USA	Iowa
Admission to Union	NA	December 28, 1846
Land Area (in square miles)	3,537,438.44	55,869.36
Population Total	308,745,538	3,046,355
Population Density (people per square mile)	87.28	54.53
Population Percentage Change (April 1, 2000, to April 1, 2010)	9.7%	4.1%
White Persons (percent)	72.4%	91.3%
Black Persons (percent)	12.6%	2.9%
American Indian and Alaska Native Persons (percent)	0.9%	0.4%
Asian Persons (percent)	4.8%	1.7%
Native Hawaiian and Other Pacific Islander Persons (percent)	0.2%	0.1%
Some Other Race (percent)	6.2%	1.8%
Persons Reporting Two or More Races (percent)	2.9%	1.8%
Persons of Hispanic or Latino Origin (percent)	16.3%	5.0%
Not of Hispanic or Latino Origin (percent)	83.7%	95.0%
Median Household Income	$52,029	$49,007
Percentage of People Age 25 or Over Who Have Graduated from High School	80.4%	86.1%

*All figures are based on the 2010 United States Census, with the exception of the last two items.

How to Improve My Community

Strong communities make strong states. Think about what features are important in your community. What do you value? Education? Health? Forests? Safety? Beautiful spaces? Government works to help citizens create ideal living conditions that are fair to all by providing services in communities. Consider what changes you could make in your community. How would they improve your state as a whole? Using this concept web as a guide, write a report that outlines the features you think are most important in your community and what improvements could be made. A strong state needs strong communities.

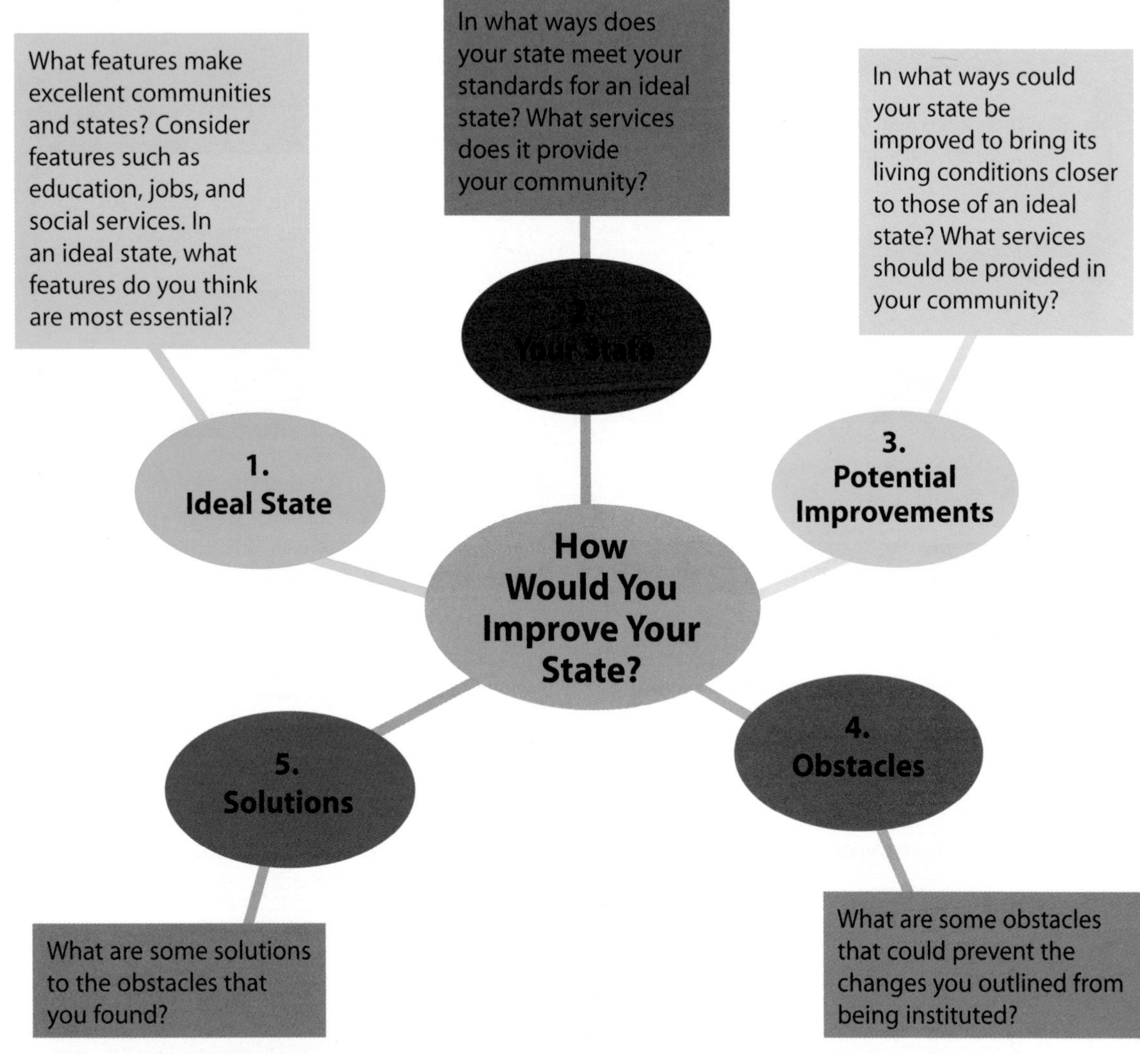

What features make excellent communities and states? Consider features such as education, jobs, and social services. In an ideal state, what features do you think are most essential?
In what ways does your state meet your standards for an ideal state? What services does it provide your community?
In what ways could your state be improved to bring its living conditions closer to those of an ideal state? What services should be provided in your community?
2. Your State
1. Ideal State
3. Potential Improvements
How Would You Improve Your State?
4. Obstacles
5. Solutions
What are some solutions to the obstacles that you found?
What are some obstacles that could prevent the changes you outlined from being instituted?

Exercise Your Mind!

Think about these questions and then use your research skills to find the answers and learn more fascinating facts about Iowa. A teacher, librarian, or parent may be able to help you locate the best sources to use in your research.

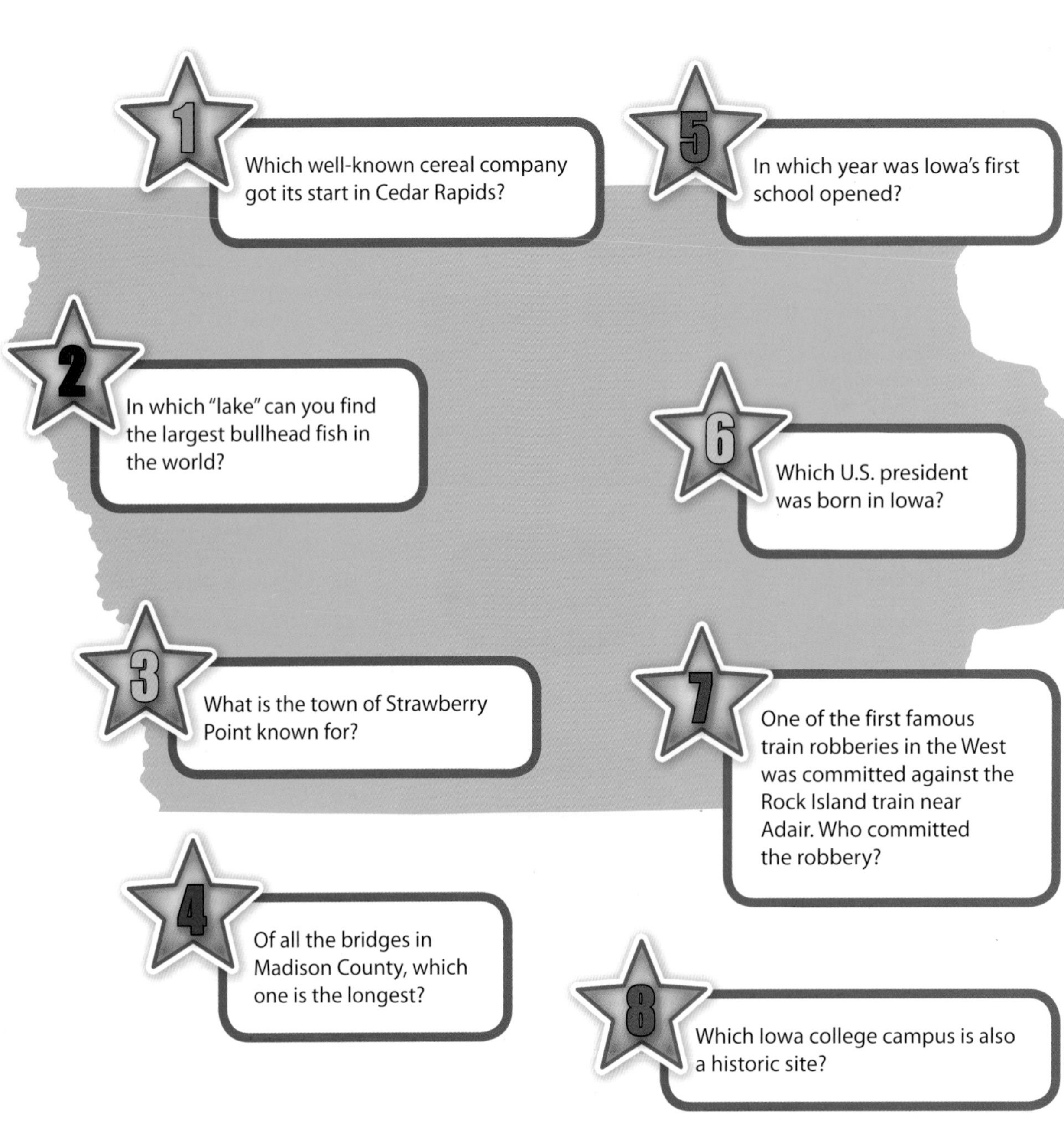

1
Which well-known cereal company got its start in Cedar Rapids?
2
In which "lake" can you find the largest bullhead fish in the world?
3
What is the town of Strawberry Point known for?
4
Of all the bridges in Madison County, which one is the longest?
5
In which year was Iowa's first school opened?
6
Which U.S. president was born in Iowa?
7
One of the first famous train robberies in the West was committed against the Rock Island train near Adair. Who committed the robbery?
8
Which Iowa college campus is also a historic site?

Words to Know

biodiesel: a substitute for diesel fuel made from vegetable oil

communal: a type of lifestyle in which all items and possessions are shared within a community

endangered: in danger of dying out

ethanol: a form of alcohol that can be used as a fuel in automobiles

extinct: died out

game: wild animals hunted for food or sport

genetics: the study of how characteristics are passed down from generation to generation

glaciers: large masses of slow-moving ice

grassroots: developed at the community or local level

Great Depression: a huge decline in the world economy that lasted from 1929 until 1939, with widespread unemployment and poverty

hybrid: a plant or animal that is a combination of two different plants or animals

Louisiana Purchase: a large area purchased from France by the United States in 1803

Mormon: a follower of a religion founded by Joseph Smith in 1830

persecution: being attacked for one's beliefs

pilgrimage: a journey made to a place of worship

primaries: elections to choose candidates to run in the general election

renewable: a resource that can be used over and over without being depleted

reserves: supplies

suffrage: the right to vote

watershed: a line of separation between waters flowing to different river basins

windbreaks: trees or bushes that are planted to provide shelter from the wind

yields: the amount of a crop produced by cultivation per unit of land area

Log on to www.av2books.com

AV² by Weigl brings you media enhanced books that support active learning. Go to www.av2books.com, and enter the special code found on page 2 of this book. You will gain access to enriched and enhanced content that supplements and complements this book. Content includes video, audio, web links, quizzes, a slide show, and activities.

Audio
Listen to sections of the book read aloud.

Video
Watch informative video clips.

Embedded Weblinks
Gain additional information for research.

Try This!
Complete activities and hands-on experiments.

WHAT'S ONLINE?

Try This!

Test your knowledge of the state in a mapping activity.

Find out more about precipitation in your city.

Plan what attractions you would like to visit in the state.

Learn more about the early natural resources of the state.

Write a biography about a notable resident of Iowa.

Complete an educational census activity.

Embedded Weblinks

Discover more attractions in Iowa.

Learn more about the history of the state.

Learn the full lyrics of the state song.

Video

Watch a video introduction to Iowa.

Watch a video about the features of the state.

EXTRA FEATURES

Audio
Listen to sections of the book read aloud.

Key Words
Study vocabulary, and complete a matching word activity.

Slide Show
View images and captions, and prepare a presentation.

Quizzes
Test your knowledge.

AV² was built to bridge the gap between print and digital. We encourage you to tell us what you like and what you want to see in the future.

Sign up to be an AV² Ambassador at www.av2books.com/ambassador.